Thinking Music Method

PRIMER
by **Ruben De Anda**

Dedication

> "When I am playing music,
>
> I am not **thinking** of anything else."
>
> **- Raul De Anda**

Contents

Brief History

CHAPTERS

A Brief History

I wrote this book for musicians who want to understand music on a deeper level and for those students who want a good path to follow to learn music.

My father was an industrial mechanic at a copper refinery. He describes his career this way: "If it was broke, I'd fix it. If there was a problem, I'd have to build a solution." After teaching many students and fixing their many mistakes, I discovered a solution to the common problems with current methods developed for teaching music.

Most methods for learning music teach students where to place their fingers and how to read music notation, but they don't reveal how the music was composed. In high school guitar class, we learned how to read music without being taught any music theory. Because I found music fascinating, I continued to learn one piece of music after another hoping that one day I would understand what was going through the composer's mind when they created music.

In college, I struggled to find the answers in my lessons. Because I couldn't, I thought that either I had missed out on an earlier music education lesson in grade school, or I had some sort of music learning disability. My music theory class had interesting lessons about music, but my desired revelation of "how do I think like Mozart" remained elusive.

The educational system I experienced seemed to be created on this premise:

You have to learn music *before* you can learn music.

College music classes required many prerequisites before students could take music composition. The prerequisite classes were full of how to read and other knowledge, but I wanted to hone my composing skills. I felt like I would be left behind by the time I got to music composition. Frustrated, I dropped out and continued my own self study. This conundrum continued until I finally had an instructor at a community center who used an inventive way of teaching how to improvise music. That's when I had the breakthrough moment on how to train myself to think like Mozart. I started to develop a method that provides a definite starting point on the journey to music mastery.

I took an objective look at how music is organized and started to analyze what the most common aspects were and developed exercises to help my fingers, ears, and brain understand them.

Though I have not attained mastery myself, I can tell you exactly where I am and what steps I'm taking to improve my skills. With the Thinking Music Method, you too will be able to see the clear path to your goals and where you are each step of the way. It is not easy, but having a map with clear sign posts that indicate how far you have traveled makes for an easier journey.

I designed these books to give you the clearest understanding of what all musicians are doing when they get up and play their instrument, whether they are conscious of it or not. Each book builds upon the lessons of the previous books.

So, select the book that corresponds with your favorite instrument, and let's get started. If you want to learn how to play guitar, the Thinking Music Method: Guitar Edition is the perfect place to start.

Introduction

CHAPTER 1

Introduction

Welcome!

We see them, we hear them, we know it is music that they play, but what exactly is going on in their minds? What magic are they casting? How does one become a musician? In order to begin to think like a musician, one must know what a musician does.

A musician is an artist of sound. A musician vibrates objects to produce sound waves. By weaving together certain sound waves, a musician creates invisible structures of sound that fill moments of time for the listener.

By comparing artists and the way they manipulate their medium, we can begin to grasp musicians' thoughts.

This book introduces the concepts of harmony, key, scale, major scale, beat, meter, and measure. The various types of popular musical instruments are also introduced.

A visual artist manipulates color on a canvas to create a painting. By studying color theory, shapes, and painting techniques the painter becomes a master painter.

A cook manipulates flavors to create dishes. By studying the culinary arts, and practicing cooking techniques the chef becomes a master chef.

A musician manipulates sound waves to create music. By studying music theory and mastering techniques the musician becomes a Maestro.

Knowing exactly what one wishes to achieve

makes it easier to achieve it.

Why this method works

There are many methods of learning how to play music. Some students are taught to play pieces of music either by reading music or by mimicking the actions of their teacher. They are taught one musical composition after another without any instruction as to how the pieces were composed. Other people teach themselves to play music by mimicking what they hear on recordings and not fully understanding how the composer created such works.

Thinking Music Method (TMM) differs from other methods because it exposes you to the way music is structured, much in the same way a student of visual art is first exposed to the basics of color harmony or the way a beginning Spanish student learns the most common Spanish phrases. By providing you with foundational concepts to analyze music, the seeds of understanding how music is structured can take hold faster and grow quickly and strong. TMM offers context through music exercises and examples to help you know exactly where you are on the journey of achieving mastery.

Learning about music should be a wondrous personal journey. Set a direction and explore to your heart's content. Don't worry about how you compare to other musicians. Care about what you have learned, and continue to grow your skills.

Your journey into music has been organized in TMM books to take you through the following steps:

 **Step 1** Learn how music is structured. This includes understanding basic harmony and rhythm, and the vocabulary used to describe different pieces of music.

 **Step 2** Learn how your instrument is used to play music. This includes proper use and techniques of your choice of musical instrument.

 **Step 3** Learn how to improvise music. Being creative with a newly learned musical concept gives you the ability to put new concepts into practice.

 **Step 4** Learn how music is notated. It is not absolutely necessary to read music, but it will help your brain organize musical exercises from easiest to more difficult.

 **Step 5** Learn more complex concepts and apply them. After you understand the new concept, incorporate it into your improvisational practice.

By gradually introducing more complex concepts, you will increase your knowledge and, by applying that knowledge to musical exercises, you can benefit by improvising more complex music.

Each book in the TMM expands on these steps, gradually increasing in complexity as you progress through them.

Harmony

CHAPTER 2

Harmony

Sandra De Anda

> **"** Think not of what you see,
> but what it took to produce what you see. **"**
> - **Benoit Mandelbrot**

This chapter will cover the concepts of harmony, key, musical scale, and major scale.

Many of the things that we perceive as being beautiful, or in musical terms "harmonious", come from simple proportions.

To demonstrate how proportions are used in music, we will prepare your mind by first seeing how proportions are used to create visual beauty. Pleasing proportions are usually constructed from simple forms.

This logo of a lightbulb by Andrew Becker is the result of a process that begins with a simple square.

Andrew Becker

Step 1 A simple square is drawn.

Step 2 A square of the same size is placed next to it.

Step 3 A square with a width of the two squares is placed next to the two squares.

Step 4 A square with a width of the small square and the larger square is placed next to the grouping of squares.

Step 5 A square with a width of the previous two squares is placed next to the grouping of squares.

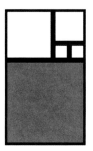

Step 6 Finally a square with a width of the previous two squares is placed next to the grouping of squares.

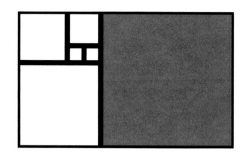

Step 7 Simple circles are drawn within the squares. This creates a ***structural framework*** that can be used to make beautiful pictures.

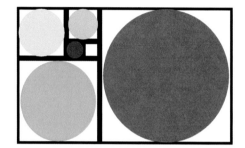

We now have shapes of pleasing proportions that the mind can play with. By keeping the **relative proportions** we can have more <u>confidence</u> in designing something pleasing, knowing that they come from the **same framework.**

Andrew Becker

A logo is created with
pleasing proportions.

Here are some examples of using simple proportions to create pleasing logo designs.

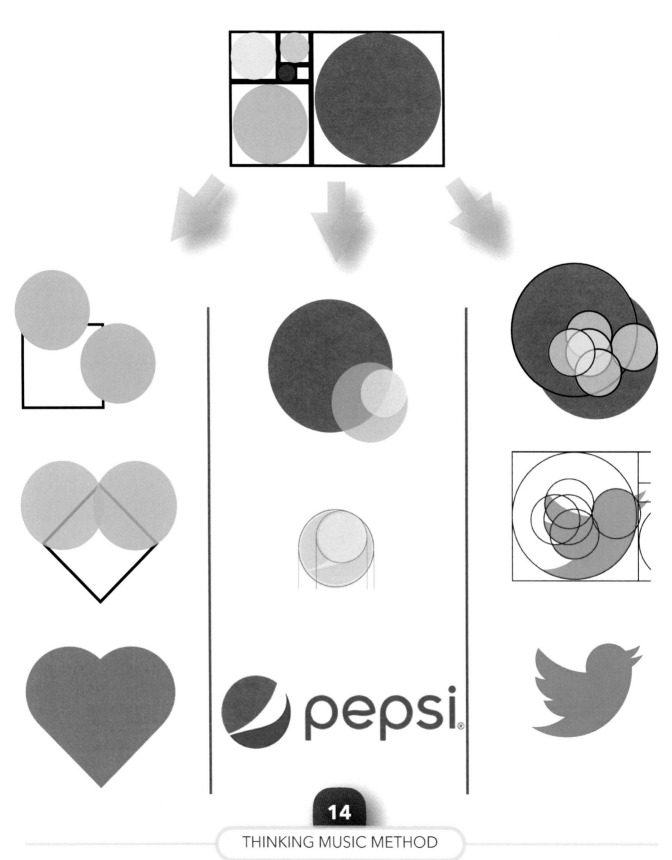

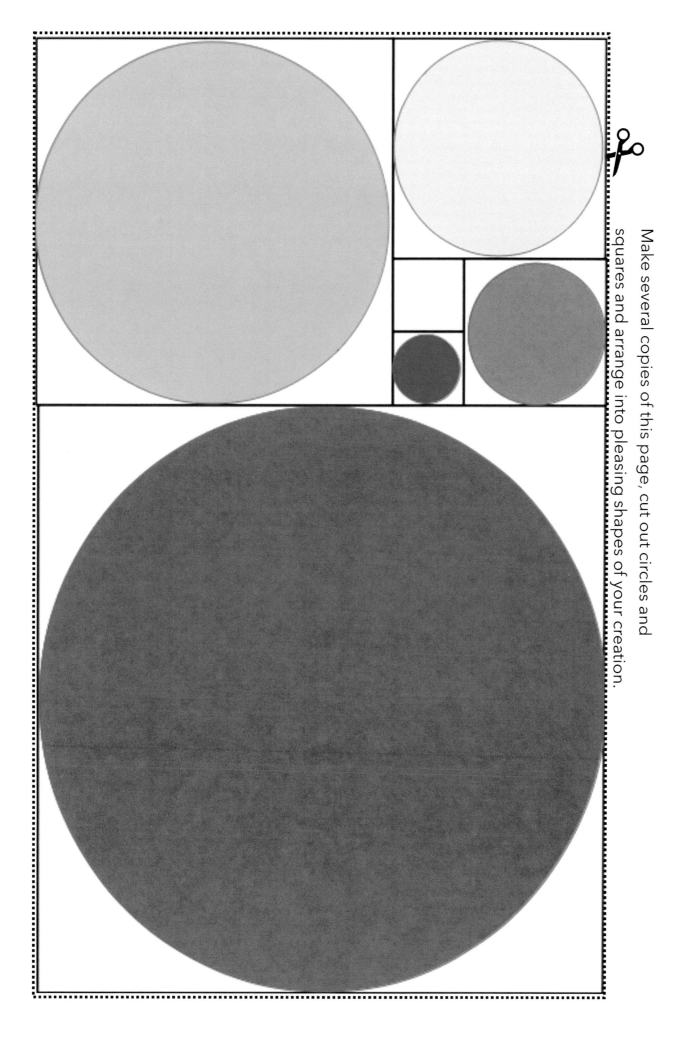

Make several copies of this page, cut out circles and squares and arrange into pleasing shapes of your creation.

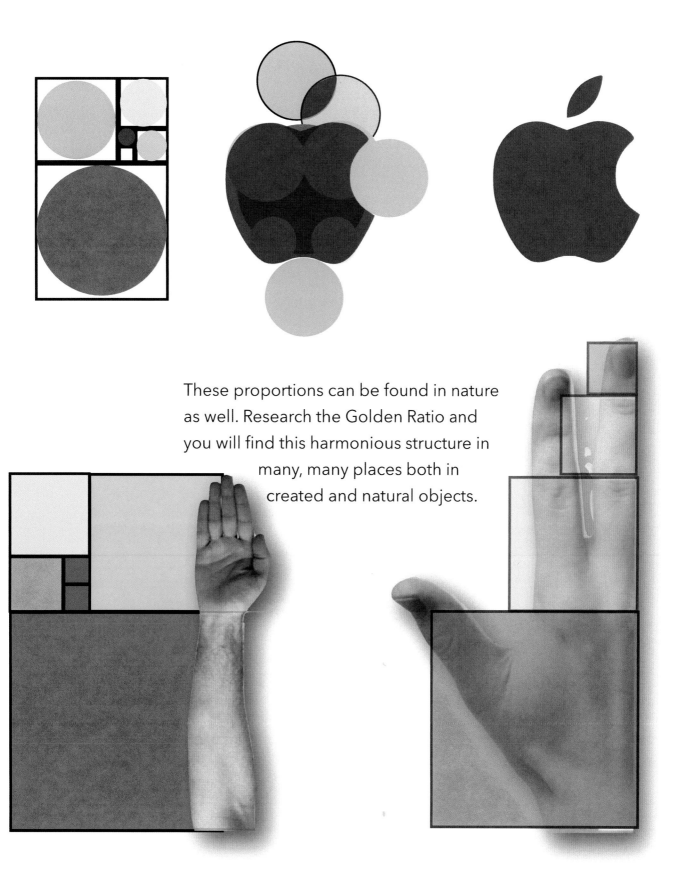

These proportions can be found in nature as well. Research the Golden Ratio and you will find this harmonious structure in many, many places both in created and natural objects.

This visual analogy of beauty derived from simple proportions helps prepare your mind for understanding musical harmony. Many of the sounds we hear are perceived as beautiful because they are most commonly derived from simple proportions.

Harmony in music is derived from a simple single sound wave much like the initial simple square.

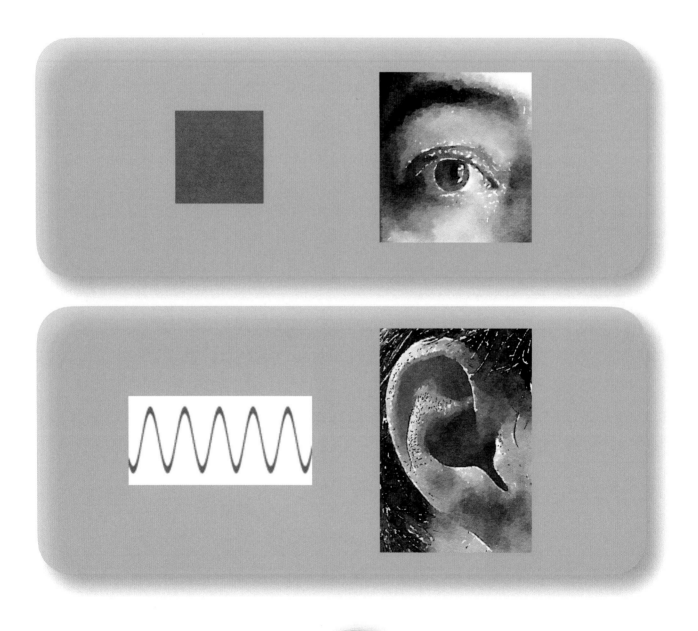

Sound waves

**Think not of what you hear,
but what it took to produce what you hear.**

Sound waves are very fast vibrations moving through the air. The rate of the vibration is called the frequency. A sound wave with a specific frequency is referred to as a note in music.

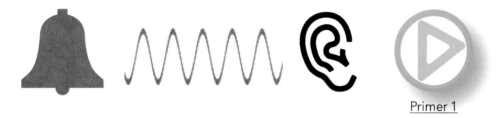

Primer 1

By simply doubling the frequency of one note, we create a second wave that sounds different than the original wave.

 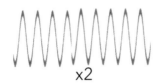 

x2

Primer 2

 These play buttons allow you to listen to the audio examples throughout my digital books. Please visit soundcloud.com username Thinking Music Method. The direct link is: https://soundcloud.com/user-47217242-526012947 or visit www.ThinkingMusicMethod.com

When we listen to both of these notes simultaneously, we perceive **harmony**.

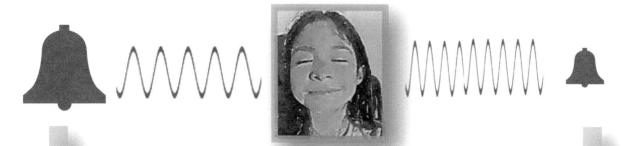

Harmony is two or more sound waves or notes played at the same time that sound pleasing to the ear.

key

key x2

Having established a **Key** note and its double, we now have two notes. Imagine the notes as two points on a line.

At this point imagine that there can be any number of different notes between the Key note and its double. Some of these notes will harmonize with the Key. Most of them will not harmonize.

A **musical scale** is any number of specific set notes that include the Key note and notes found between the Key note and its double. A musical scale is a **structural framework** used to make music, similar to the squares and circles used to make the light bulb logo.

One musical scale has proportions of notes so beautiful that it has has been used in billions of compositions in all worldly cultures since the year of the soup. The proportions of this scale are so beautiful that it makes most humans wish they knew how to play a musical instrument. The musical scale that you will study for the rest of your life is known as the...

THINKING MUSIC METHOD

Major scale

The Major scale consists of notes that have proportions that are simple ratios of the key note. They are approximately located on the half, one fourth, one third, two thirds, one eighth, and seven eights of the *distance* between the Key and key x2.

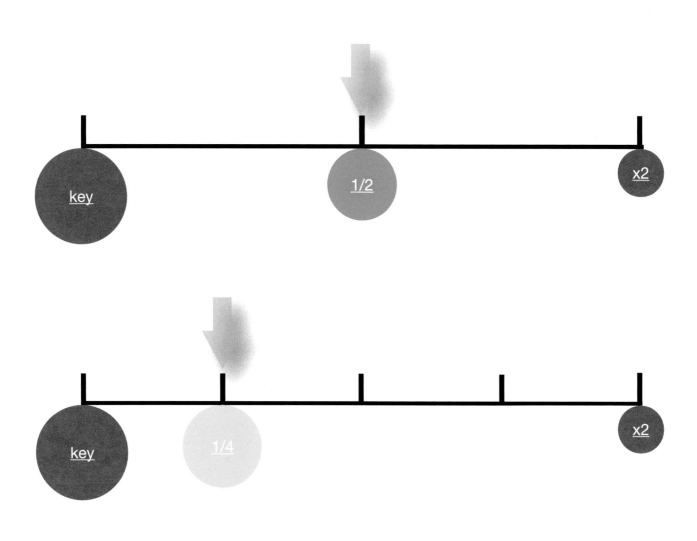

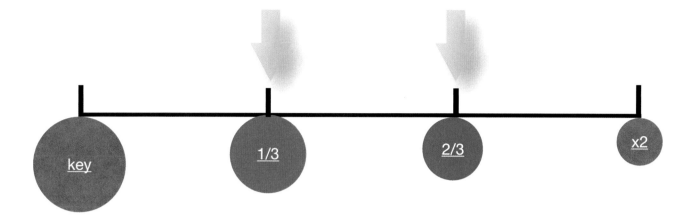

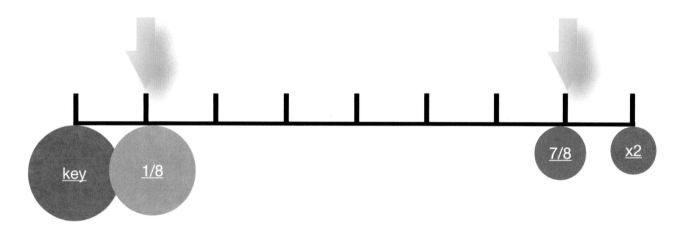

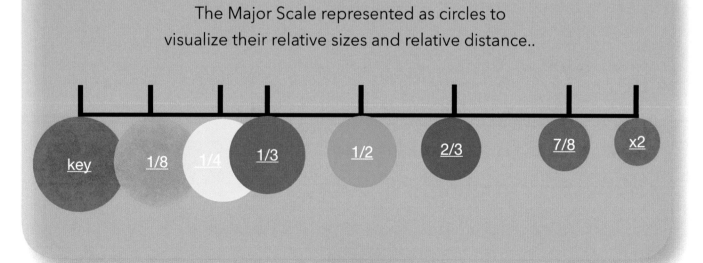

The Major Scale represented as circles to visualize their relative sizes and relative distance..

THINKING MUSIC METHOD

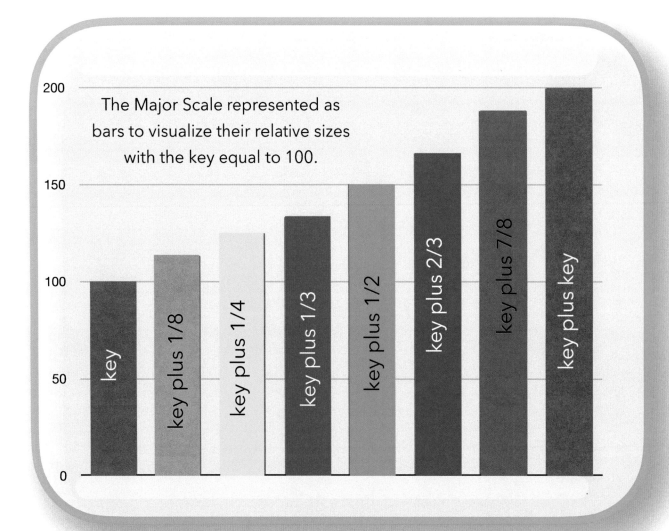

The Major Scale represented as bars to visualize their relative sizes with the key equal to 100.

- key
- key plus 1/8
- key plus 1/4
- key plus 1/3
- key plus 1/2
- key plus 2/3
- key plus 7/8
- key plus key

For those who have a fear of fractions, it is not necessary to memorize the exact fractions. However, it will be crucial to learning the labels that have been assigned to each of these fractions in the next lesson.

These specific fractions exist in the natural world as well as in human music. Virginia Morell wrote in her article for ScienceMag.com, "Birds found using human musical scales for the first time" on Nov. 3, 2014, "The flutelike songs of the male hermit thrush (*Catharus guttatus)* are some of the most beautiful in the animal kingdom. Now, researchers have found that these melodies employ the same mathematical principles that underlie many Western and non-Western musical scales"

The famous American composer, Irving Berlin learned how to play the Major Scale on his piano and used it to compose all his music. Some of his most popular songs are *Cheek to Cheek, White Christmas, God Bless America, Blue Skies, There's No Business Like Show Business, and Puttin' on the Ritz.*

Because it is difficult calling out fractions while playing music, musicians have labeled the fractions with letter names. The Gregorian Monks are the ones credited for assigning the first seven letters of the alphabet to these notes. Their affinity for using the note located at 2/3 in the scale in their music, led them to label this 6th note as the "A" note. "A" being the first letter of the alphabet. The Key x2 is given the same letter name of C, because of its similarity in sound to the original. I am omitting it for now to avoid confusion as I explain other musical concepts, but will explain this further in Book 2 in the Intervals Chapter.

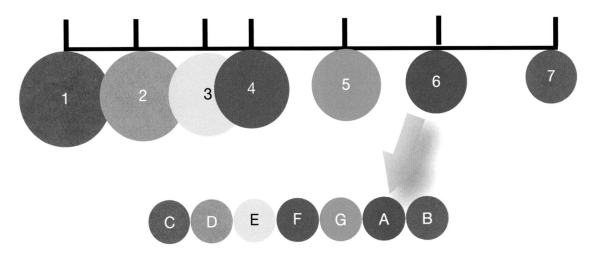

The rest of the notes were labeled like this.

Some cultures use other methods of labeling the notes of the major scale. For example the Solfege system uses these syllables to represent the notes of the Major Scale.

Do Re Mi Fa Sol La Ti

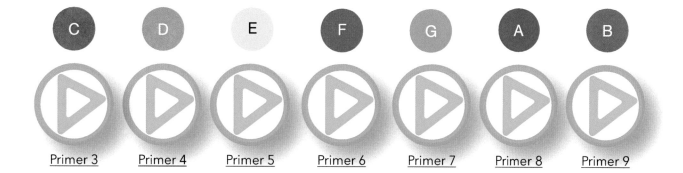

C	D	E	F	G	A	B
Primer 3	Primer 4	Primer 5	Primer 6	Primer 7	Primer 8	Primer 9

Here is an opportunity to listen to the notes. At this point I encourage you to refer to the *Thinking Music Method Instrument Book* to learn how your musical instrument produces these notes.

The musical alphabet consists of these letters **A B C D E F G.**

Practice saying these letters out loud:

ABCDEFG ABCDEFG ABCDEFG ABCDEFG

Then practice saying the letters backwards:

GFEDCBA GFEDCBA GFEDCBA GFEDCBA

Later, being able to say these letters in sequences will help your brain learn musical sequences easier.

These are some common sequences found in music:

1. **ABC BCD CDE DEF EFG FGA GAB**

2. **ACE CEG EGB GBD BDF DFA FAC**

3. **ABCD BCDE CDEF DEFG EFGA FGAB GABC**

4. Now say the previous sequences backwards.

CHALLENGES

AHEAD

Rhythm

CHAPTER 3

Beat

Playing music is about playing the right note at the right time. **Rhythm** is the organization of moments of time used to indicate when and when not to play notes. The first concept in understanding rhythm is the **beat**.

tap   tap   tap   tap

the Beat

The **beat** is the sensation of a continuous pulse felt when listening to music. Foot tapping to music usually occurs on the beat.

In an orchestra the conductor visually tells the other musicians when the **beat** occurs.

In a rock band the drummer audibly tells the other musicians when the the **beat** is occurring by hitting the drums.

Tempo

The beat can occur slowly or quickly. The speed at which the beat pulses along is referred to as the **Tempo**.

Beats are measured in units of Beats Per Minute. 40 beats per minute or 40 B.P.M. is a slow tempo and 200 B.P.M. is a fast tempo.

The Italians labeled ranges of B.P.M. using words such as Largo, which is a slow tempo approximately ranging from 40 B.P.M. to 60 B.P.M. and Presto, a fast tempo of about 180 B.P.M. to 200 B.P.M.

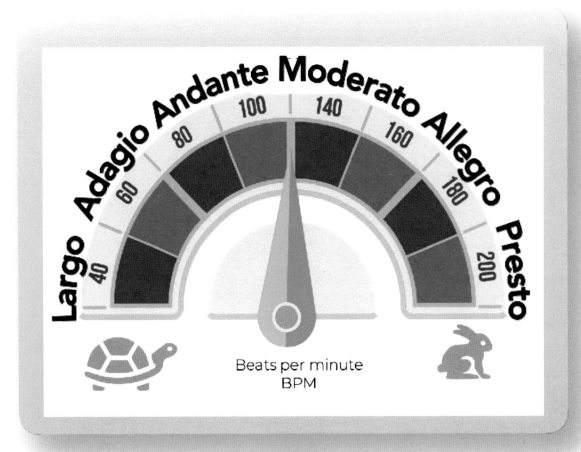

Largo Adagio Andante Moderato Allegro Presto

40 60 80 100 140 160 180 200

Beats per minute
BPM

Here are some examples of a beat at different beats per minute.

Largo
50 B.P.M

Primer 10

Andante
100 B.P.M

Primer 11

Moderato
120 B.P.M

Primer 12

Presto
180 B.P.M

Primer 13

THINKING MUSIC METHOD

Being able to have a good sense of keeping time is another skill a musician must have. Having a machine that you can practice with is highly recommended. The most common is the metronome. Metronomes used to be a clockwork device but now an app on the phone will do the same function. I prefer to use drum machines to keep time because they are less tedious to listen to and more fun. Some electronic keyboards have drum machines built in. YouTube also has thousands of videos of metronomes or drummers keeping time. Search for 90 B.P.M. and you will find various videos of different styles of percussionists to help you keep time.

metronome app

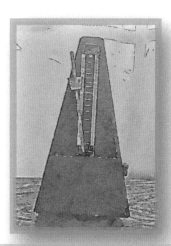

classic metronome

electronic keyboard with built in drum machine

When the brain learns a new skill, connections between areas of the brain are created. As this new skill is repeated, the brain coats the connections with more myelin. Myelin works as a type of insulation that makes the signal travel faster between these areas of the brain. More repetitions means more myelin. More myelin means the skill can be executed faster than before the repetition. By applying this knowledge of how myelin works to the practice session, musicians can practice music more efficiently.

Using a metronome to keep a slow tempo helps musicians focus on the accuracy of the new musical skill. Once accuracy is obtained then the tempo can be increased, and increased, and increased. There seems to be no limit as to how fast the brain can execute a well practiced skill.

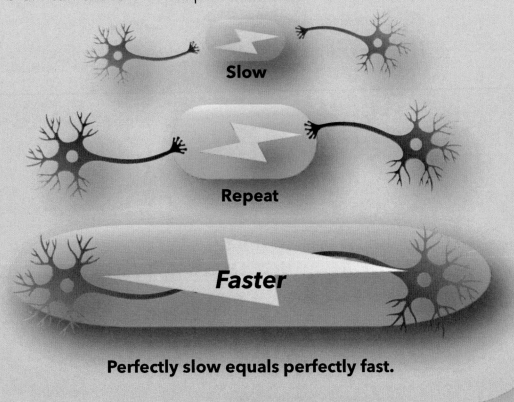

Slow

Repeat

Faster

Perfectly slow equals perfectly fast.

Measure

Beats can be either **accented** (loud or strong) or **unaccented** (soft or weak).

Beats are arranged in groups of accented and unaccented beats. These groups are called **measures**. The measure is defined visually with two vertical lines called **bar lines** on either side of the groupings of beats. Here are several examples of accented and unaccented beat combinations. The accented beat is most commonly first.

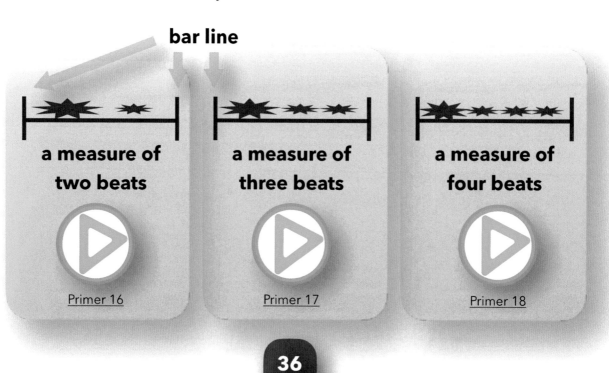

Different groupings within a measure are referred to as the **meter**. Meters of 4, 3, and 2 are the most commonly used and make up about 80 to 90 percent of popular music. It is most common for a piece of music to have multiple measures with the same number of grouped beats in each measure.

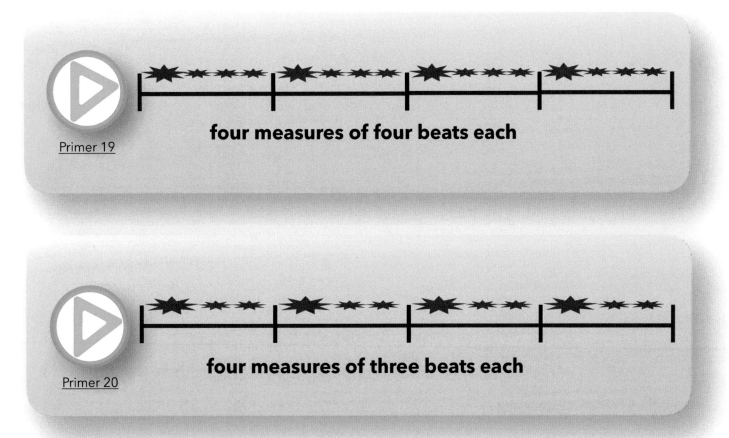

Primer 19

four measures of four beats each

Primer 20

four measures of three beats each

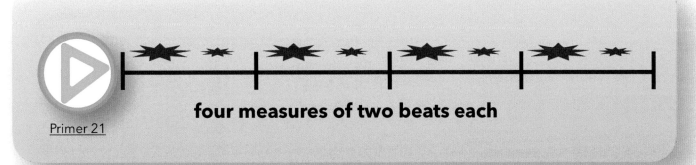

Primer 21

four measures of two beats each

The average pop song is 3 minutes long. The average Tempo of a song is 108 B.P.M. The most common beats per measure is 4. Therefore a traditional song will have about 81 measures. This is what 81 measures with 4 beats each would look and sound like.

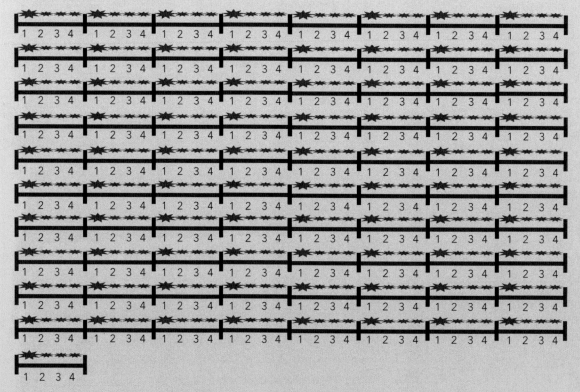

Primer 22

Read aloud every number in the above 81 measure example. Tap your foot along with the drum sound at the same time.

If this is too difficult at first, keep trying until you can do this easily.

Playing music requires mental discipline. This type of training will help you later on your musical journey when you want to play something more difficult. The following compositions have someone counting the beat by saying "1234" at the beginning of the song. This is known as the "count in". Pick a song you are familiar with and try continuing the count through the entire song.

1, 2, 3, 4

40 - U2

A Matter Of Trust - Billy Joel

Baby I'm a Star - Prince

Ball Of Confusion (That's What the World Is Today) - The Temptations

Bombs Over Baghdad (B.O.B.) - OutKast

Can't Get Enough - Bad Company

Crazy Mama - J.J. Cale

Daniel - Bill Ryder-Jones

Don't Bring Me Down - Electric Light Orchestra

Fulton County Jane Doe - Brandi Carlile

Future Politics - Austra

Get Up - James Brown

Give Peace A Chance - John Lennon

Good Lovin' - The Young Rascals

Goodbyes - Jorja Smith

Hey Ya - OutKast

Honey, We Can't Afford to Look This Cheap - The White Stripes

I Just Want to Celebrate - Rare Earth

I Saw Her Standing There - The Beatles

Instant Replay - Dan Hartman

It's Kinda Funny - Josef K

Let's Dance - Chris Montez

Meet Me in the Hallway - Harry Styles

Paradise - Bazzi

Play - Marmozets

Pretty Fly (For A White Guy) - The Offspring

R.A.M.O.N.E.S. - Motörhead

Raspberry Beret - Prince

Red Solo Cup - Toby Keith

Reggatta de Blanc - The Police

Rhythm Nation - Janet Jackson

Roadrunner - The Modern Lovers

Romeo - Chairlift

She Looks Like Fun - Arctic Monkeys

Slip Kid - The Who

Taxman - The Beatles

The Ocean - Led Zeppelin

Three Packs a Day - Courtney Barnett

Turn It On Again - Genesis

Vertigo - U2

Walls - Tom Petty & the Heartbreakers

Wooly Bully - Sam the Sham & the Pharaohs

You Got Lucky - Tom Petty & the Heartbreakers

Instruments

CHAPTER 4

Musical Instruments

The purpose of a **musical instrument** is to produce the notes of a major scale. A drum is not a musical instrument because it does not produce notes. A drum is a percussive, rhythmic instrument. Violins, pianos, trumpet, guitar, and harmonica are some examples of musical instruments because of their ability to play a major scale. Some instruments require more skill to produce notes than others. Playing a note on a piano is very easy as compared to a trumpet.

Your choice of which instrument to start with is up to you. If you have a personal attraction to the sound of the trumpet, then try it. If you want the easiest instrument to play, the piano or keyboard requires very little effort to push on a piano key to produce a note. If you want easy and portable, then a stringed type of instrument may be to your liking.

If you feel confident in your computer skills, then you might want to try using a computer to play your compositions. It is possible to compose music using a computer without having to learn how to play a musical instrument. There are music composing programs that can play digital sounds of many musical instruments.

Excluding the human voice and computer, most musical instruments are categorized into roughly three categories

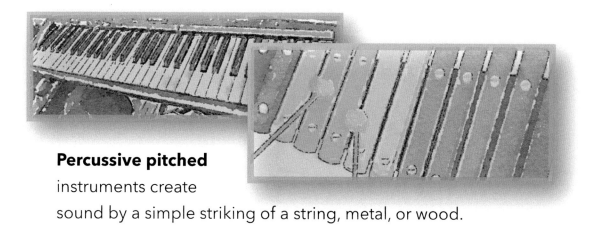

Percussive pitched
instruments create
sound by a simple striking of a string, metal, or wood.

Stringed
instruments create
sound either by plucking, bowing, or
strumming the string.

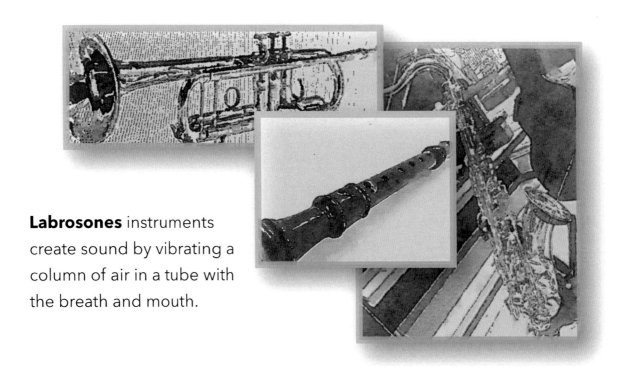

Labrosones instruments create sound by vibrating a column of air in a tube with the breath and mouth.

The **computer** is a useful tool used in many aspects of music making. It can notate scores, synthesize the sound of any instrument and record music. I have even seen the computer use artificial intelligence to compose music. The following are the websites and applications that I have used to help further my music career and used to help students with their progress.

Youtube

I have had many students tell me they tried using YouTube to learn how to play guitar and found it to be very confusing. There are countless musicians on this platform and together they probably have billions of lessons. The problem is that students don't have enough knowledge about music to know where to start. Many music teachers on YouTube use musical terminology incorrectly, making it more difficult to use this site effectively.

Once a student has a better grasp of music harmony, then I introduce using YouTube videos as a tool. I first direct them to my channel (Ruben De Anda) and show them the playlists I have created to help them practice. Playlists are organized by the same concepts that are covered in TMM Book 1. For example, the "One Chord Backing tracks" playlist has a collection of music that only has one triad, and they are all related to the key of C.

Other playlists are videos that have useful information about the world of music.

Lumbeat is a channel that I share with students who prefer to listen to a drummer as opposed to a metronome to keep the beat.

Looper for YouTube is a Google chrome extension that gives the ability to repeat specific sections of a video. With the speed settings control, this can be used to impressive effect in learning a piece of music.

 **Noteflight** is a website that has an online music notation program. It is free to use and is $49 to access all the features.

 **iRealPro** is an application that can generate a virtual band to practice with. Input a chord progression, select the tempo, and style and you instantly have a full band to practice scales or arpeggios with.

 **Bandlab** is a social music recording platform that is great for collaborating with other musicians from anywhere around the world.

 **Midiguitar** is an application that converts your guitar input into a polyphonic keyboard synthesizer. Which means you can make your guitar sound like any musical instrument making practice more enjoyable. Sound like a piano one day and a violin the next.

Levels of enjoyment with music.

Listening to recorded music.

Listening to live music.

Playing someone else's compositions for yourself.

Playing others' compositions by yourself for a live audience.

Playing others' compositions with other musicians.

Composing your own music.

Playing your compositions for a live audience.

Playing your compositions with other musicians for a live audience.

Improvising music with musical friends on a lovely Sunday afternoon.

According to "How Music Bonds Us Together," by Jill Suttie, "Researchers recently discovered that we have a dedicated part of our brain for processing music, supporting the theory that it has a special, important function in our lives. Listening to music and singing together has been shown in several studies to directly impact neuro chemicals in the brain, many of which play a role in closeness and connection. Now new research suggests that playing music or singing together may be particularly potent in bringing about social closeness through the release of endorphins."

Once you choose which instrument you want to try, get the corresponding *Thinking Music Method* book that will introduce how that instrument is commonly used to make music. A brief history of that instrument and proper techniques on how to play it are included in its book. My goal is to have these books published by 2023.

The Thinking Music Method Desk Bells is designed for the parent with some or no musical training, who wishes to introduce music to their child to give them a head start. It is filled with games and exercises to help young minds start musical ear development.

I have personally used desk bells to teach my students music theory concepts with great success. The ability to move the bell notes around into different configurations really helps to visualize the musical concepts discussed in the TMM Book.

Review

CHAPTER 5

" There is no learning without remembering. "

- **Socrates**

Quiz

1. Harmony is _____ or _____ notes that sound pleasing when played together.

2. Any number of specific set notes that include the Key note and notes found between the Key note and its double is a _____.

3. The speed at which the beat is pulsing along is referred to as the _____.

4. Beats are arranged in groups of accented and unaccented beats in what are called _____.

5. Learning music is _____.

6. The first _____ letters of the Alphabet are used to label the different notes of the major scale.

7._____ instruments create sound either by plucking, bowing, or strumming the string.

8. A musical instrument is designed to play _____ scales.

9. A tempo of 160 beats per minute will be in the _____ range.

10. A machine that can produce a steady beat is called a _____.

Summary

Here are the terms taught in this Primer. Please make sure you have a grasp of these terms, because everything that follows is based upon them.

Music is the arrangement of **sound waves** and their ratios over a period of time, where harmony and rhythm combine.

Musicians use musical instruments to produce sound waves.

Notes are sound waves with specific frequencies.

The **Key** refers to one specific starting note where all the other notes are derived from.

A **musical scale** is composed of notes that relate to one Key note.

The **major scale** is the most popular musical scale.

The major scale notes are labeled with the letters **CDEFGAB.**

A **beat** is a constant pulse felt in music.

Beats can be **accented** or **unaccented**.

A **measure** is a group of accented and unaccented beats.

Meter refers to the number of beats in a measure. A piece of music will have several measures with the same meter.

Print and cut out these flashcards and study them daily.

Key	Notes
Musician	Musical Scale
Major Scale	Beat

Notes are sound waves with specific frequencies.

Key refers to one specific starting note where all the other notes are derived from.

A **musical scale** is composed of notes that relate to one Key note.

Musicians are people who use musical instruments to arrange notes in durations of time.

A **beat** is a constant pulse felt in music.

The **major scale** is the most popular musical scale.

Rhythm	Tempo
Measure	Music
Meter	Harmony

Tempo is the speed at which the beat pulses along.

Rhythm is the organization of moments of time used to indicate when and when not to play notes.

Music is the arrangement of sound waves and their ratios over a period of time, where harmony and rhythm combine.

A **measure** is a group of accented and unaccented beats.

Harmony in music, is two or more sound waves or notes played at the same time that sound pleasing to the ear.

Meter refers to the number of beats in a measure.

I hope this book helped give you insight to the invisible structures that are used in music. Having these concepts in mind will help you on your journey to becoming a musician.

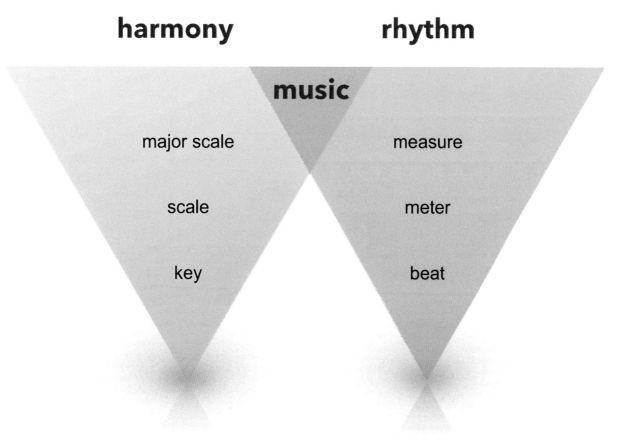

harmony   rhythm

music

major scale   measure

scale   meter

key   beat

The Primer introduces you to basic musical concepts. Choose the instrument book that corresponds to your instrument of choice. Continue your journey thorough books 1,2, and 3. More musical examples that will prepare you for the world of music are in my Tune Books.

THINKING MUSIC METHOD

Index

Thank you!

Thank you to all my music teachers and to all my music students.

Thank you to all who helped contribute to this book especially:

Leticia S. De Anda

Norma De Anda Nguyen

Sandra De Anda

Linda Bannan

Mike Bannan

Nina Hofstadler

Francisco Antonorsi

Christy Johnson, editor catalystchristy@gmail.com

Support

Ruben lives with his wife and cat in Southern California. He has brought a love and deeper understanding of music to numerous students. Donations to support this work and expanding series can be directed to…

https://www.patreon.com/RubenDeAnda

or

my PayPal account: deandaguitar@gmail.com

Thank you!

Made in the USA
Las Vegas, NV
04 November 2022

58757313R00045